Introduction

Having traveled the World as a Naturalist, Artist and Dive Guide, I have enjoyed Wonderful encounters with some of Natures most spectacular achievements.

From Botswanas Okavango River Delta to the Rain Forest of Australias Tropical North I have sought out the Dynamic Wildlife and landscapes that make these places compelling and unique.

It is my hope that future generations will have these same opportunities to be awestruck by our natural world.

T-Rex

T-Rex - Jake, you seem troubled!

Jake - I am! So many of my Animal friends are having a difficult time and I am wondering what I can do to help.

T-Rex - Having experienced extinction I can tell you that it is very serious and last forever. I think now is a good time to go find out what the issues are and what the solutions might be.

Jake - That's a Great Idea! That's what I will do!

TORTOISE

Jake - You seem to move very slowly through life, is that helpful?

Tortoise - Yes ! and it has served us well.

We have lived along side the Dinosaurs and Crocodilians for Millions of years and like the Crocodiles we have ushered in many new worlds.

When the Planet changes slowly animals have the time and opportunity to adapt.

But when the Planet changes quickly (like the current rate of climate change) Animals cannot keep pace and they disappear.

Whatever you can do to protect and preserve the Health of the Planet will benefit the future of all living things.

Elephant

Jake - Why do they say "memory like an Elephant"?

Elephant - Because our big families are led by a Matriarch that has the responsibility for the welfare of all members.

Sourcing food and water over hundreds of miles with changing seasons and changing climate requires an incredible memory.

To accomplish this we use ancient migratory routes that are proven to supply our needs, but more and more it means navigating humans which makes it much more difficult.

Killer Whale

Jake - What's it like as one of the Oceans Top Predators?

Killer Whale - It can be very difficult!

If the Ocean is not healthy do to Over Fishing, Pollution or Climate Change, those problems impact the entirety of the food chain and get magnified towards the top.

It will benefit all life forms at all levels to protect our Oceans. They are after all, the foundation of Life.

SLOTH

Jake - Didn't Sloths look very different many thousands of years ago?

Sloth - That's true, we use to be very large ground dwelling herbivores. As the Planet changed, we changed and became arboreal (tree dwellers) and totally dependent on Tropical Rain Forest.

We are not alone. Tropical Rain Forest support some of the richest biodiversity on this Planet and also act as its lungs by purifying the air that we breathe.

Camel

Jake - Why have you chosen such a harsh place to live?

Camel - It's not for everyone Jake. The ability to live in this Desert heat with very little water requires adaptations over hundreds of thousands, if not millions of years.

With your current rate of climate change you are turning more of your Planet into Desert without that time to adapt.

This is a hard place to make a living Jake and I would recommend that you do what's needed to avoid it.

Orangutan

Jake - The name Orangutan is unusual, what does it mean?

Orangutan - It means Person of the Forest. In fact, we are primarily arboreal (tree dwellers) that rely on large unbroken stands of Indonesian Rainforest to supply our food and shelter.

We are specifically designed to move through the trees and we use them like highways in the sky to conduct our lives.

When our Jungle home becomes fragmented by Palm Oil Plantations or other forms of Deforestation we become isolated, making it difficult to find food and shelter as well as our friends and family.

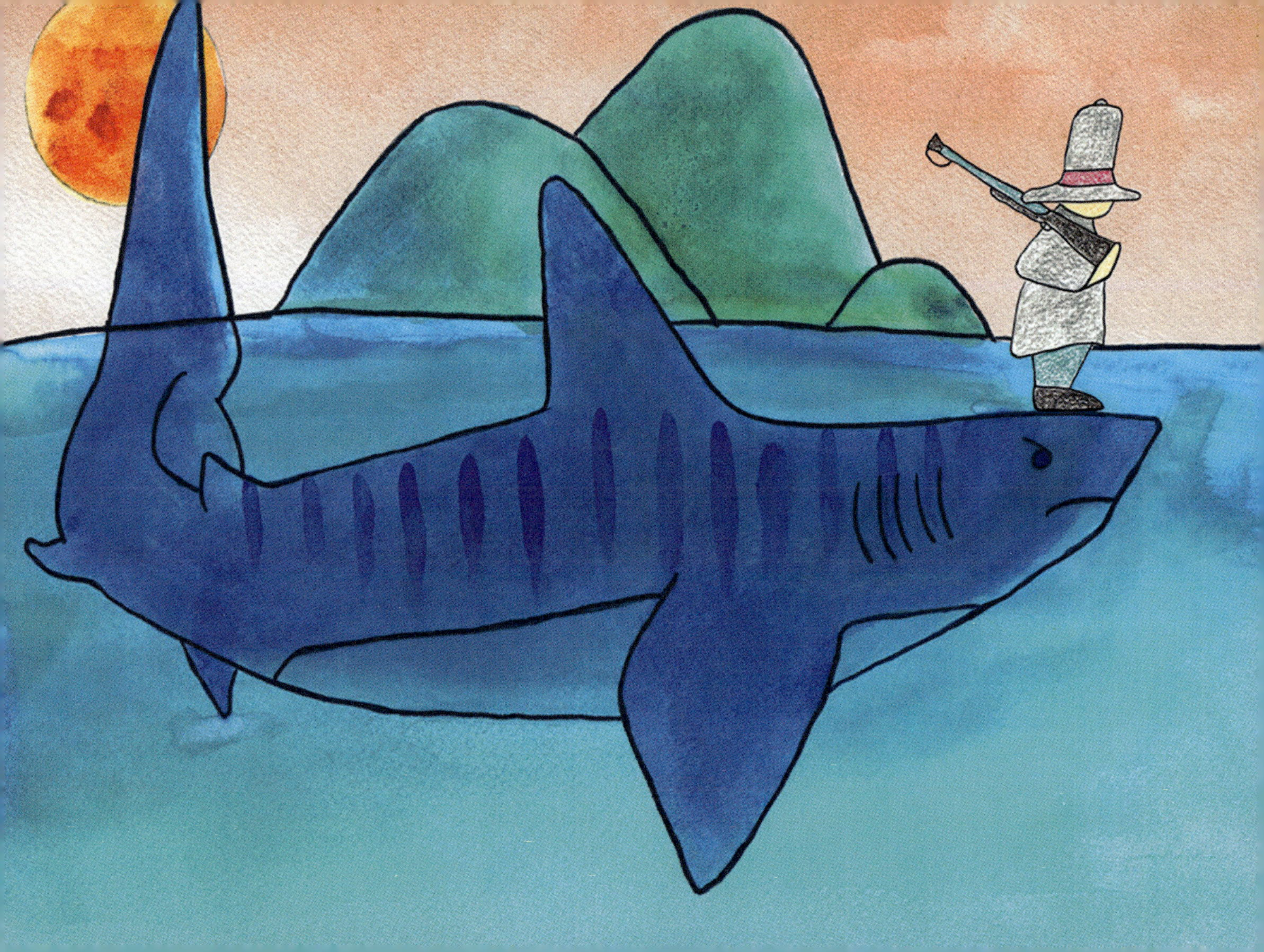

SHARK

Jake - Why are people so afraid of Sharks?

Shark - I don't think most people understand how important we are to the health of the Ocean.

Unfortunately we are over fished for Shark Fin Soup and our absence in the food chain will affect the overall vitality of the Seas.

It would benefit the Ocean greatly if people would stop eating Shark Fin Soup and restore the proper balance to our aquatic ecosystem.

CASSOWARY

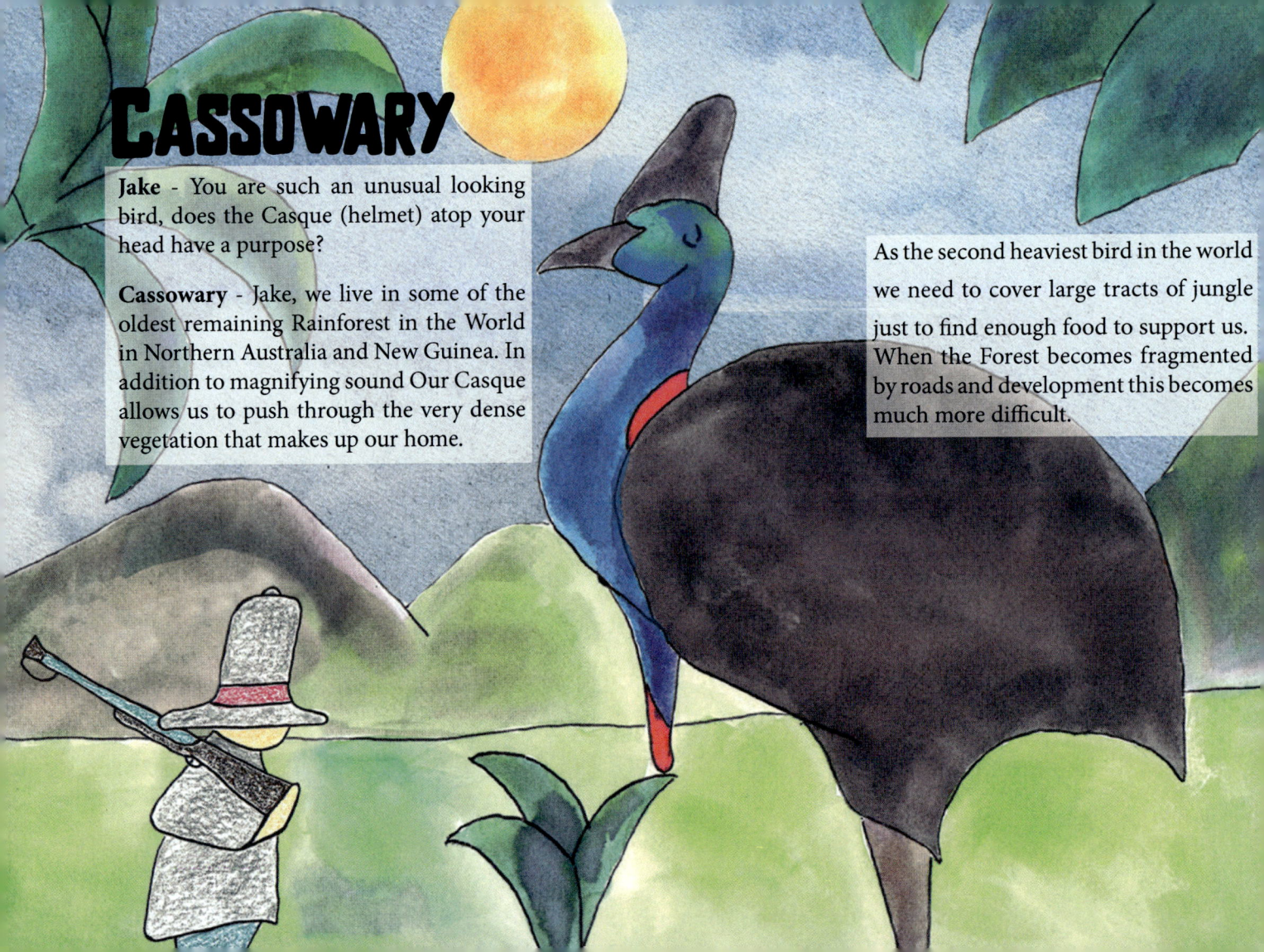

Jake - You are such an unusual looking bird, does the Casque (helmet) atop your head have a purpose?

Cassowary - Jake, we live in some of the oldest remaining Rainforest in the World in Northern Australia and New Guinea. In addition to magnifying sound Our Casque allows us to push through the very dense vegetation that makes up our home.

As the second heaviest bird in the world we need to cover large tracts of jungle just to find enough food to support us. When the Forest becomes fragmented by roads and development this becomes much more difficult.

MANATEE

Jake - Is it true that you are related to Elephants?

Manatee - Yes, we are distant cousins and we are both gentle plant eaters.

While Elephants roam the savannas and woodlands to accommodate their big appetites we travel the warm coastal waterways in search of the sea grasses that are a big part of our diet.

It is really important to us and other Sea Life that coastal areas, particularly Mangrove Forest, are protected as they are the nursery for the Ocean and provide vital protection to to the Coastlines.

OKAPI

Jake - You look a lot like a funny Giraffe.

Okapi - We are the Rainforest Giraffe!

Even though we are a big animal our color pattern allows us to disappear into the Equatorial African Jungle.

We share this home with other dynamic wildlife like Gorillas and Forest Elephants. We all need expansive pristine forest to provide the food and shelter that is critical to our survival.

Buffalo

Jake - Where did all of the Buffalo go?

Buffalo - There use to be millions of us across the Plains and Woodlands of North America. We were a very important part of Native American Culture and survival.

Now we are finally recovering from the early days of Western settlement and exploitation. But Jake, we have along way to go and we need a healthy plains ecosystem to go back to.

SUMATRAN RHINO

Jake - You look very different from other Rhinos!

Sumatran Rhino - We are!

We are the Smallest and most ancient of the five Rhino Species. They call us the "Hairy Rhino". Our size allows us to move through the dense jungle habitats of Indonesia where we make our home.

However, we do share the same concerns as all other Rhinos with our Horns sought after for the myth of medical cures.

When coupled with Deforestation/Habitat Loss we are very close to the brink and very much need human intervention on our behalf.

CROCODILE

Jake - How long have Crocodiles been around?

Crocodile - We have lived right alongside of the Dinosaurs and have watched the Planet change dramatically over the last 100 million years.

We have seen many species come and go but recently the changes have been more rapid and severe.

For us to enjoy another 100 million years we need humans to protect the climate that has produced the beautiful waterways that we all rely on.

Saber Tooth

Jake - What changed with the "Ice Age"?

Saber Tooth - Frozen land bridges connected Continents and allowed animals and people to migrate to new territories.

It was also when we first encountered Humans. In the begining we didn't pay much attention but eventually their big brains created tools that allowed them to out compete us for food and resources.

Only the Animals that could navigate Humanity survived.

Humpback Whale

Jake - Aren't you glad that the Barbaric days of Whaling are over with.
Humpback Whale - If only that were true. Unfortunately there are still Countries that are guilty of this Cruel Practice.
While we appreciate your reverence for Whales, there is still a lot more you can do. Primarily, Protect the health of the Ocean and pressure those Countries that are still Whaling to Stop.

Malayan Tapir

Jake - What is Nature's Strategy behind your unusual appearance?

Malayan Tapir - Our Unique disrupted color pattern works as Great camouflage in the dappled light of our Malaysian Rainforest Home.

This design protects us and keeps us well hidden but is only effective if our Jungle Home stays intact.

We need your help to protect these Important Ecosystems that have produced so many unique animal species like ourselves.

Musk Ox

Jake - "You look like an Ancient Animal !"

Muskox - Yes! Along with Bison and Pronghorn Antelope we made the long journey from the Pleistocene (Ice Age) into the Modern Day.

We traveled frozen land bridges that no longer exist into the Arctic where the Tundra provides food and habitat similar to our Ice Age home.

Even though we are a relic from the distant past we hope that Humans will help us into the future by protecting the Climate and preserving our Tundra Home.

Komodo Dragon

Jake - How did you grow to be such a large lizard?

Komodo Dragon - We are a product of Island Evolution. Our remote archipelago provided us with the isolation needed to achieve Gigantism.

When we arrived on these Islands they were void of large land predators and we grew to fill that void.

This isolation can be problematic as well leaving us vulnerable to human encroachment, invasive species and climate change. With your help we will continue our reign over this Primeval World.

GORILLA

Jake - What type of Ecosystem supports the largest of the Great Apes?

Gorilla - Our Rainforest home in Equatorial Africa provides well for us as long as it remains undisturbed.

We use our imposing size and strength to navigate the dense tangle of Jungle that keeps us safe and well fed.

As gentle plant eaters we enjoy a peaceful existence and we would very much like to keep it that way!

Giraffe

Jake - The view must be Great from up here?

Giraffe - It is! we can survey the Savanna for as far as the eye can see which helps us avoid danger.

It's what we can't see that concerns us. Like all African Wildlife we rely on Seasonal Rains to produce the vegetation that sustains us.

With a changing climate there is now uncertainty about when and if these rains will fall and the availability of food and water. Our future depends on a healthy climate that produces predictable rains.

Hippopotamus

Jake - I understand that the name Hippopotamus translates to "River Horse."

Hippopotamus - Yes, that's true, maybe because we run and bounce along the bottom of waterways rather than swim.

Or because all aspects of our lives are so inextricably linked to the Rivers and Lakes that make up our home.

Our total dependence on water and seasonal rains makes us very vulnerable to drought so we hope that humans work hard to Protect the Climate for all of us.

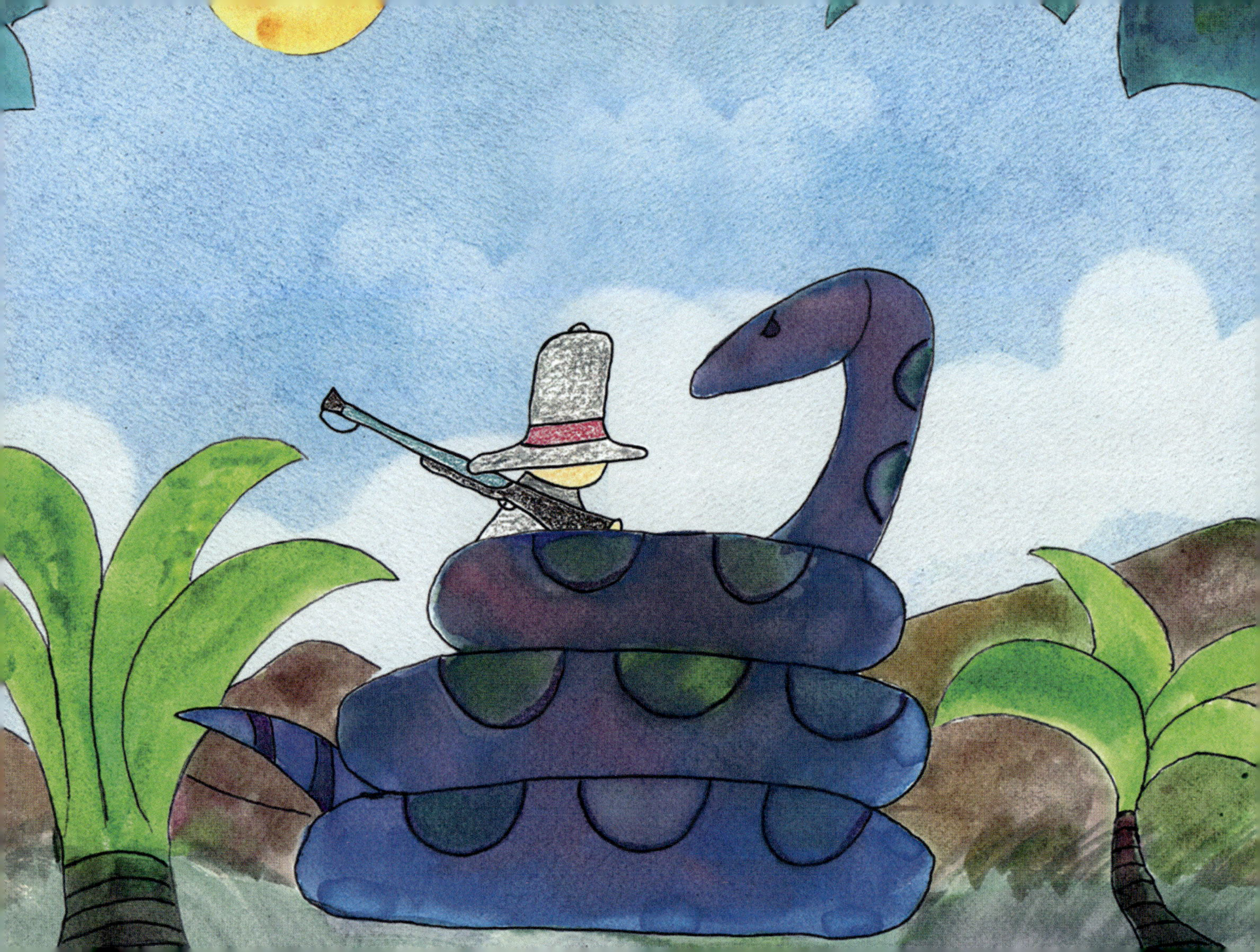

Python & Cobra

Jake - Why are Snakes so misunderstood?

Cobra - The whole Adam and Eve story got us off to a bad start with people.

Python - In reality, we are not evil, we are very shy and we do everything we can to avoid conflict with humans. That is the primary purpose of our myriad of elaborate designs and warning signals.

More than anything else we just want to be left alone.

LION

Jake - Is life easier as the King of the Jungle?

Lion - You would think so, but it can be very challenging. We require a lot of space and food to accommodate our big social families. People have many of the same needs and it is a balancing act whenever we share a home.

Furthermore, we are threatened by the Senseless practice of trophy hunting.

Please let people know that Animals are much more Majestic in the wild or on film than mounted on a wall.

Rhino

Jake - Is it true that you survived the Ice Age?

Rhino - Yes, we are an ancient animal that has lasted thru eons of different climates and humans.

Now we struggle with people taking our Horns for the myth of medical cures promoted by traditional medicines.

In reality our horns are made Keratin just like your fingernails and have no medical value at all. It is our hope that education will put an end to these cultural practices and guarantee us a future

Sea Lion

Jake - It looks like fun to be a Sea Lion!

Sea Lion - Most of the time it is a lot of Fun! We love to ride waves and play hide and seek in the Kelp Forest.

What's not fun is when we get caught in the things that people leave in the Ocean like fishing nets and plastics.

We also worry about the future of our kelp forest which are diminished by a rapidly changing climate.

Since all of our futures are tied to a healthy Ocean and Climate we hope that humans take better care of both.

Polar Bear

Jake - Mr Polar Bear, you look Very Uncomfortable.

Polar Bear - I am Jake, as the Ice Bear we rely on large Arctic Ice flows to hunt and make our homes. As the planet warms and the ice flows disappear so do our homes and food.

Jake, we can't be the Ice Bear without Ice. So anything you can do to protect the Climate will benefit the Arctic and help to insure both of our Futures.

CHIMPANZEE

Jake - You seem very familiar!

Chimpanzee - That's because we have shared much of the same evolutionary journey.

Our genetics are so similar that we have been used in product testing and space travel to insure human safety.

Now we need your help to preserve our African Rainforest home by preventing Drought, Deforestation and Human Encroachment.

Sea Turtle

Jake - You have swam these Oceans for Millions of years, what has changed?

Sea Turtle - Plastics and Garbage are a recent introduction into our aquatic world with very negative results.

Our survival requires Clean Oceans and Clean Nesting Beaches free of debris and development.

For our ancient lineage to continue we need humans to respect and revere the Oceans for the important Life Source that they are.

Hornbill

Jake - Why are there so many different looking Hornbill species?

Hornbill - That's because we occupy very different habitats that each require special adaptations.

Unfortunately specializing makes animals very vulnerable to abrupt Environmental changes like Deforestation, Drought and Fires all of which we need your help to avoid.

MOAI

Jake - What happened here at Easter Island?

Moai Head - Like all Islands, we only have the resources that exist here.

When those resources are gone, they are gone forever.

Jake, your Planet is a Beautiful Island in the Universe and you need to treat it like the very precious place that it is.

Wallaby

Jake - What makes Australia such a unique place?

Wallaby - We have benefited from millions of years of geographic isolation. It has created a Continent full of wildlife that exist nowhere else in the World.

However, this isolation makes us vulnerable to invasive species (animals that don't belong) like cats, rats, and cane toads.

To protect our Wonderful Wildlife heritage we need to preserve these lands that are the source of our creation.

WALRUS

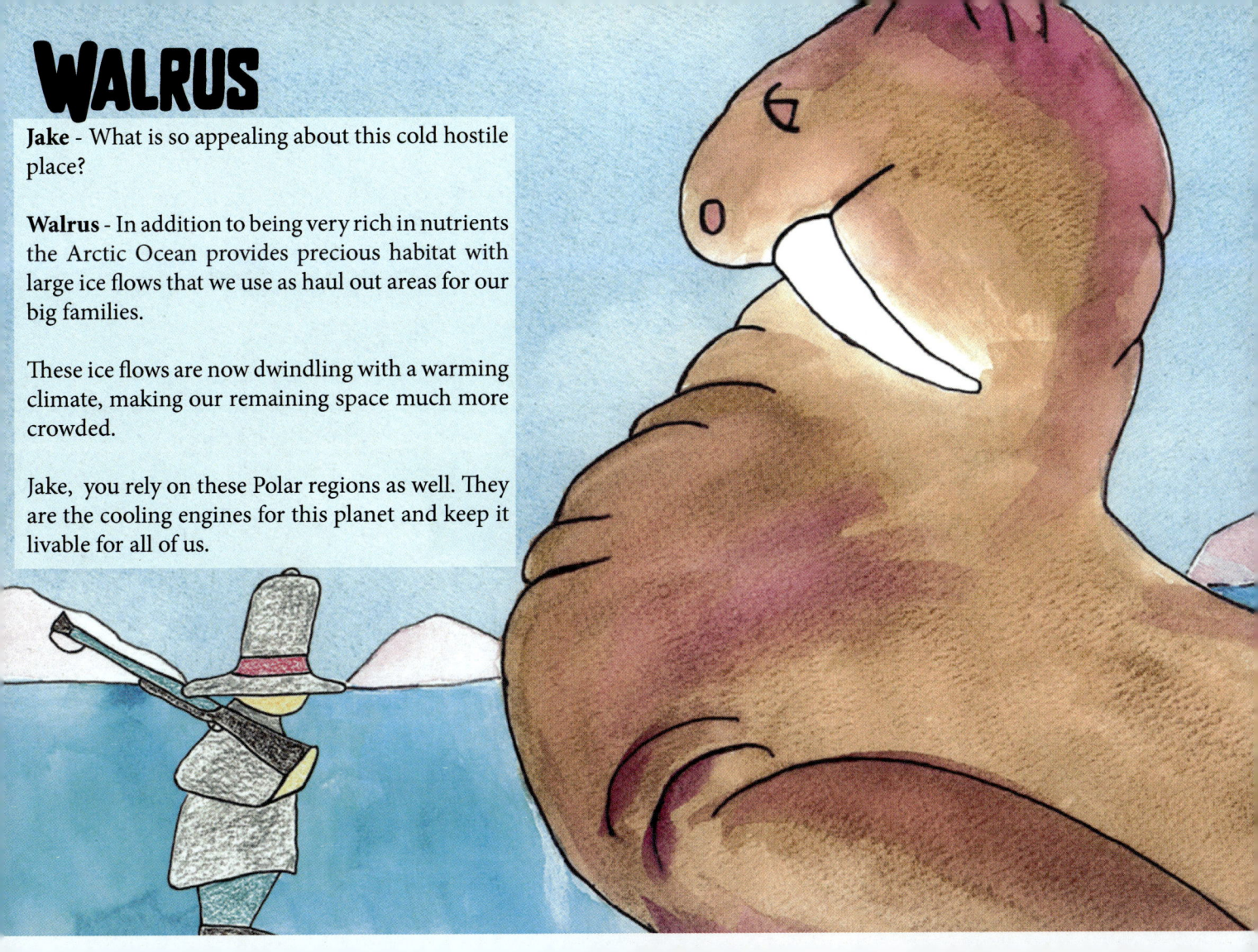

Jake - What is so appealing about this cold hostile place?

Walrus - In addition to being very rich in nutrients the Arctic Ocean provides precious habitat with large ice flows that we use as haul out areas for our big families.

These ice flows are now dwindling with a warming climate, making our remaining space much more crowded.

Jake, you rely on these Polar regions as well. They are the cooling engines for this planet and keep it livable for all of us.

PANGOLIN

Jambo Jake - Why are Pangolins having such a difficult time?

Pangolin - The Myth of medical cures!
Traditional medicines have had a profound negative impact on Wildlife populations around the World.

Much like Rhino horns our scaly plates are made of keratin (just like your fingernails) and are sought after for health remedies when in fact they have no medical value at all.

As termite eaters we protect the trees and hope that people recognize our vital role in maintaining a Healthy Ecosystem.

Tree Kangaroo

Jake - What's a Kangaroo doing way up here?

Tree Kangaroo - While our terrestrial cousins were forced to the ground by a drying Continent. We kept to the trees in these remaining pockets of ancient Rainforest.

We are now so specialized for this cloud forest habitat that any changes in this landscape are difficult for us. These regions are an important link to our primeval past as well as a critical part of our future.

Manta Ray

Jake - As the smartest fish in the Ocean, what are your concerns?

Manta Ray - like all plankton filter feeders (including Whales) we depend on Clean & Productive Oceans, rich in nutrients and free of debris.

We would also like to be able to glide peacefully through our aquatic universe without fear of harvest for the trade in traditional medicines.

JAVA RHINO

Jake - You are a hard Rhino to find!

Java Rhino - That's because there are not very many of us.

While we use to be widespread throughout Asia, we are now confined to the remote jungles of a single Indonesian Island.

Our future is very uncertain and largely depends on the protection and preservation of our last remaining home.

DRILL MONKEY

Jake- Do these remote pockets of African Rainforest provide you and your family with all of the resources you need?

Drill - Our arboreal and terrestrial search for food and shelter keeps our troops constantly on the move. We depend heavily on undisturbed jungle, free of human encroachment, to meet our needs.
We Greatly appreciate the efforts of people (Liz & Pete) who work hard to protect these areas and Champion our survival.

PENGUIN

Jake - Why are these Polar Regions so Important?

Penguin - They are critical in regulating our Planet's temperature and keeping it livable for all of us.
They are also instrumental in the production of the crustacean krill, which is a vital part of the Marine food chain.

No matter where you live on this Planet, you benefit from healthy Polar Regions.

PYGMY HIPPO

Jake - It seems unusual to find such a small Hippo in these remote regions of Rainforest.

Hippo - Your Right ! Our range is very limited to only a few Countries in Equatorial Africa.

Unlike our Big Gregarious cousins who occupy many open waterways, we prefer a solitary existence in dense marshy habitats far removed from human activity.

Borneo Pigmy Elephant

Jake- Aren't You kind of small for an Elephant?

Pigmy Elephant- We are the smallest sub species of Asian Elephant.

Our isolated evolution on the Island of Borneo regulated our growth to match the available resources.

We now face the challenges presented by the recent introduction Palm Oil Plantations.

This new landscape will require further adaptations on our part and the understanding and appreciation on the part of humans.

JAGUAR

Jake - What does the Worlds most powerful cat (pound for pound) need to survive.

Jaguar - Lots of Pristine Habitat!

As a secretive cat of the shadows we require large territories with thick cover and plenty of prey to make a living.

It becomes much more difficult for us when livestock and agriculture invade our previously wild home.

Like all Big Cats we depend on the ongoing protection and availability of Wild Places.

Andean Condor

Jake : You almost seem too big to fly!

Condor : We are, the Largest Flying Bird!
We rely on both thermal and dynamic soaring to stay aloft and cover the vast distances needed to find food.

It use to be much easier in the ancient days of Mega Fauna, with abundant large prey and very few people.

To survive now, we must travel much further and work hard to avoid the perils of human activity.

Terror Bird

Jake - What is the source of your imposing name?

Terror Bird - It would have to be our size and ferocity which also gave us a very long reign as the regions top predator.

However, this did not last. After millions of years the climate and competition changed and we disappeared.

This pattern has repeated itself throughout the history of this Planet and should be a cautionary tale for all those that follow, Nothing last forever.

BRONTOSAURUS

Brontosaurus - What have you learned from your journey Jake?

Jake - I have learned that our precious Planet is at an Environmental tipping point.

We need to make every effort to restore the reverence for Nature that guarantees us all a Future. This means protecting our life source, The Oceans, from Over Fishing, Pollution and Climate Change.

It means protecting both Tropical and Temperate Forest which hold much of the Worlds biodiversity while at the same time acting as it's lungs by purifying the air we breathe.

Most importantly, it means changing our behavior and avoiding products and actions that are harmful to Wildlife and Ecosystem's.

We owe it to our Beautiful Planet and Future Generations to make every effort to Protect, Preserve and Restore Mother Nature.

Here's How You Can Help

Plant Milkweed for Butterflies

Plant a Tree

Recycle - Especially Plastics

Support Wildlife Conservation Organizations like the following:

International Rhino Foundation
https://rhinos.org/donate/

Panthera
Wild Cat Conservation
https://panthera.org/

Pandrillus
African Primate Conservation
https://www.pandrillus.org/contact/donate/

Adventures in Avoiding Extiction Copyright 2024 | Editorial Design by Aly Rodriguez, Dirty Desert Collective

Made in the USA
Las Vegas, NV
10 March 2025